Illumen
Winter 2025

Edited by Tyree Campbell

Illumen
Winter 2025

Edited by Tyree Campbell

Cover art "Night of the Raven" by Sandy DeLuca
Cover design by Laura Givens

Vol. XXII, No. 2   Winter 2025
Illumen [ISSN: 1558-9714] is published quarterly on the 1st days of January, April, July, and October in the United States of America by Hiraeth Publishing, P.O. Box 1248, Tularosa, NM 88352. Copyright 2025 by Hiraeth Publishing. All rights revert to authors and artists upon publication except as noted in selected individual contracts. Nothing may be reproduced in whole or in part without written permission from the authors and artists. Any similarity between places and persons mentioned in the fiction or semi-fiction and real places or persons living or dead is coincidental. Writers and artists guidelines are available online at www.albanlake.com/guidelines. Guidelines are also available upon request from Hiraeth Publishing, P.O. Box 1248, Tularosa, NM 88352, if request is accompanied by a SASE #10 envelope with a 60-cent US stamp. Editor: Tyree Campbell. Subscriptions: $28 for one year [4 issues], $54 for two years [8 issues]. Single copies $10.00 postage paid in the United States. Subscriptions to Canada: $32 for one year, $54 for two years. Single copies $12.00 postage paid to Canada. U.S. and Canadian subscribers remit in U.S. funds. All other countries inquire about rates.

New from Terrie Leigh Relf!!
Postcards From Space

Terrie Leigh Relf loves sending and receiving postcards from the four corners of the universe—and beyond! Postcards tell a story. They are mementos from friends and family—and from total strangers—and provide a glimpse into life's journeys, observations, and adventures.

Here are some messages on postcards from space, found aboard a derelict craft that crashed on an arid, lifeless world. The OSPS (Outer Space Postal Service) has delivered these messages to Terrie, who now presents them to you. This is what it is like out there.

https://www.hiraethsffh.com/product-page/postcards-from-space-by-terrie-leigh-relf

A Little Help, Please

In the world of the small indie press we fight a never-ending battle for attention to our work, as writers and in publishing. Here's an example: big publishers [you know who they are] have gobs of $$$ that they can devote to advertising and marketing. Here at Hiraeth Publishing, our advertising budget consists of the deposits for whatever soda bottles and aluminum cans we can find alongside the highways. Anti-littering laws make our task even more difficult . . . ☺

That's where YOU come in. YOU are our best promoter. YOU are the one who can tell others about us. Just send 'em to our website, tell them about our store. That's all. Just that.

Of course, we don't mind if you talk us up. We're pretty good, you know. We have some award-winning and award-nominated writers and artists, plus other voices well-deserving to be heard [not everyone wins awards, right?] but our publications are read-worthy nevertheless.

That number once again is:

www.hiraethsffh.com

Friend us on Facebook at Hiraeth Publish and follow us on Twitter at

@HiraethPublish1

Contents

Features

26	Featured Poet: Jane Stuart
33	Movie Review: Godzilla Minus One by Lee Clark Zumpe

Poems

10	The Fleur de Lys by Sandy DeLuca
12	Olduvai by Christopher Hivner
13	Astrocyte Conversion by Amanda Niamh Dawson
14	alternate route by Peter Roberts
16	A Childhood's Burden by n a spencer
17	Spaceships Found by Denny Marshall
18	The Death of Merlin by Matthew Wilson
22	I, Minotaur by A J Dalton
23	Lady of Anthropocene by Ihita Anne
31	Śrī (Skyclad) by n a spencer
32	two haiku by Denny Marshall
	Two cinquains by Richard E. Schell
38	62 Prospect Street by Sandy DeLuca
40	Dear Editor by Matthew Wilson
41	Demons by Ray Greenblatt
42	Immolation by n a spencer
44	Light the Second Sun by Amanda Niamh Dawson
45	After Mom's Divorce by Matthew Wilson
46	plenum by peter Roberts
47	Border Story by n a spencer

Illustrations

11 Belladonna by Sandy DeLuca
15 Oracle Above the River by Sandy DeLuca
19 Defeated by April Lefleur

SUBSCRIBE TO ILLUMEN!!

We'll be glad you did...
So will you.
Here's the link:

https://www.hiraethsffh.com/product-page/illumen-1

Support the small independent press!

You're not afraid of a little poetry, are you?

The Miseducation of the Androids
By William Landis

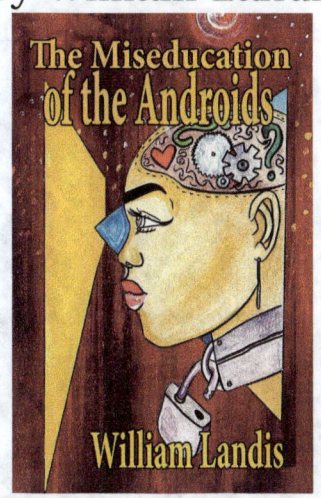

What happens when androids confront concepts inconsistent with their programming? William Landis examines this question by means of flash fiction and haiku that you will find pithy, poignant, and amusing.

William Landis is a science fiction poet from North Carolina. He is a graduate of North Carolina A&T State University, completing both undergraduate, and graduate work in agriculture. He is currently working on a vermicomposting project, and he is an Army reserve engineer officer. He enjoys running, writing, reading, and exploring new places.

Order a copy here: https://www.hiraethsffh.com/product-page/miseducation-of-the-androids-by-william-landis

Midnight Comes Early
By Marcie Lynn Tentchoff

Marcie Lynn Tentchoff lives on the west coast of Canada, in a forest of brambles and evergreens far too densely tangled to form the setting for any but the darkest of fairy tales. She writes poetry and stories that tiptoe worriedly along the border of speculation and horror, and is an active member of both the Science Fiction & Fantasy Poetry Association and the Horror Writers Association. Marcie is an Aurora Award winner, and her work has been either nominated, short, or long-listed for Stoker, Rhysling, and British Fantasy awards. She is very much involved in middle grade and YA media, and edits Spaceports & Spidersilk, a magazine aimed at readers from 8-9 up to (and past!) 89. When she is not involved with the practice of placing and editing words on a page, she teaches creative writing and acting for a performing arts studio.

Order a copy here...

https://www.hiraethsffh.com/product-page/midnight-comes-early-by-marcie-lynn-tentchoff

The Fleur De Lys...
Sandy DeLuca

I've gone there often...
on gallery tours...
art shows at close by studios
on Sunday afternoons...
shadow people follow,
mingle with art lovers...
creep near students...
or seasoned gallery guides...
a cat begging for scraps
at the top of the hill...
not many see the ghosts...
only mediums and witches...
people like me.

All of Providence is haunted...
I learned that long ago...
but I have a kinship
with Angela O'Leary...
a woman with a broken heart.

Through the years,
she's greeted me at 7 Thomas Street...
a pretty woman,
watercolor splatters on her clothes.
Her subtle smile, the way her eyes follow me...
like her portrait there.

Damn, she loved Sydney Burleigh...
her mentor...
love unrequited...
killed herself...
used gas from
her art studio's lighting fixtures.

Angela welcomes me...
scorned lover...
delicate phantom with
paint-splattered clothes.

My kind of girl.

Originally published in Phantoms of Providence

Belladonna by Sandy DeLuca

Olduvai
Christopher Hivner

The clear water flows
across the dawn
of man,
down the channels of dirt,
reddish brown diamonds
that cup the liquid
like astral carriers,
a river of stars
bleeding light
from the black
to discharge
a silvery path
for us to follow,
follow, follow,
in ancient time,
fresh dirt from the shovels
of the scientists
sprays the sky soft,
silken shifts of dust
cover our bones
as man emerges
from the caves
trailing the water
through the desert
to life
among the starfield.

Astrocyte Conversion
Amanda Niamh Dawson

Clamping down
Profound
Bounce in your step
Never forget
Lost realms
Orion's wry belt

Five points of song
Systematically prolonged
Synaptic drones
Cell overloads

Our stars
Within
Unfold

alternate route
Peter Roberts

the path of madness
like a path into woods
looks always inviting:
    dark & unknown,
    away from main roads,
    leafy & cool, filled
    with lyrical birds
    & charming animals;
    empty of people
    & pressing demands,
    a pleasant respite, a brief diversion

    but

both forest & madness
like all deviant choices
balance promise with risk:
    brambles & briars
    & poisonous plants,
    spiders in webs
    & snakes by the path;
    trails that twist,
    delude, disappear,
    'til you find no way forward,
    no way to turn back,
    & no way out, to return to your life.

Oracle Above the River
by Sandy Deluca

A childhood's burden ...
~ n a spencer

Protect your spirit, because you are in the place
where spirits get eaten ...
~ John Trudell

A childhood's burden
                         as even now
                         to know
The press of the solar wind
Touching down my shoulders

Cast out
        like some enormous shadow
Filling the sky with mercury and water

Great wings beating above the clouds
And inside my chest
                      a weight
As heavy as a stone

This leaden angel
                      impassive as the moon
Unmooring the tides from their beds in the earth

And flooding the far distance
With the sighs of falling birds
And of something absent
                         eaten away
Where a child's heartbeats once might have shored
In the coronal folds of their own amplitude

Spaceships Found
Denny Marshall

spaceship found on mars
the last departing craft crashed
fleet continued on

inhale final breaths
escaping from the surface
martian atmosphere

underground prison
dry bones in every cell
martian guards long gone

far away planet
martians waiting patiently
to return back home

strong martian sandstorm
reveals alien spacecraft
skeletons of crew

The Death of Merlin
Matthew Wilson

Even new kings must not fear dead wizards
Though hate in their souls make them linger on
I will march and fight and fall with my brothers
Beneath the gloom of arrow fire where the sun
    once shone.

Horses scream louder than men when they are dying
Tripping over spear tips in the stinking mire
Shields for only wounded men against the metal hail
While the dead wizard on the hill shouts his desire.

I would once have put my total trust in Merlin
An old man even when I was a knee high boy
But even good friends have their own dreams
And this wizard wished to have a kingdom for his toy.

The corpses he has sent my way die more than once
His spells once used for good burn my people's city
This hateful cold corpse of Merlin I once loved
Whose wormy hands command the dead devoid
    of pity.

But my mother raised her Arthur not to bow to
    wickedness
And beside a wall of shields I will do what must
    be done
To defend the living against the hate of dead things
To fight my way from out the hail into the sun.

Defeated by April Lafleur

The newest from G. O. Clark!!!
Mindscapes

G. O. Clark takes on the future in this riveting collection of poetic observations about life, the Universe, and everything else. He takes you up mountains and down valleys, and always makes you wonder about what's happening and what will happen (if we aren't careful).

Ordering links:
Print: https://www.hiraethsffh.com/product-page/mindscapes-by-g-o-clark
ePub: https://www.hiraethsffh.com/product-page/mindscapes-by-g-o-clark-2
PDF: https://www.hiraethsffh.com/product-page/mindscapes-by-g-o-clark-1

The Mayfly Moons
By Shawn Vimislicky

Fantasy poetry at its finest, with new observations on classical literature, self-discovery, the longing for a better place (hiraeth), beings swept up in events, and fantasy romanticism. Often uplifting, sometimes darker, and here and there a mix of the two extremes, this collection will thrill you, haunt you, and raise your spirits.

Print: https://www.hiraethsffh.com/product-page/mayfly-moons-by-shawn-vimislicky-2
PDF: https://www.hiraethsffh.com/product-page/mayfly-moons-by-shawn-vimislicky-1
ePub: https://www.hiraethsffh.com/product-page/mayfly-moons-by-shawn-vimislicky

I, Minotaur
A J Dalton

Some would call him
Toxic
Lacking
In anger management
Some wouldn't condemn him for his nature.
-
Curse upon a brutal father
Hidden
Alone
In labyrinthine depths
Of mind, darkness and madness.
-
Waiting – starving for
Any
Eating
Stones, bones, rats and memories
Welcome ghosts of the living.
-
I, Minotaur
I am
Guilty
Horror, fearsome myth and promise
The strength beneath the palace.
-
If a hero
Should come
Vengeful
With naked sword
All intimately fatal
I would embrace him
Like a lover
To rest at last.

Lady of Anthropocene
Ihita Anne

She spent thirty years half-living, sunk into the rug
where a dirty necropolis laid hidden underneath
beside it were bedridden children thieved of relief
Meanwhile porcelain-primped parasites ran amuck
In her pitiful life of comfort and lux
Now there's no saving a rich lady of Anthropocene.
In the world below her, the maggots intervened
They ate away at the poor and out of luck
Up above, so-called overlords
were really connoisseurs of hush money
Shameless, they broke all of what they call red tape
While a world beneath dies, the real bugs sit atop a
    high horse
Unable to breathe, the people rush for a tracheostomy
Gasping for air, they pull themselves up scrape by
    scrape

Expecting to fend off the bugs
was akin to playing dead with
vultures and hoping for round two.
Electing to spend aid sums
on Berlin trips and a silver bridge,
those smugglers wriggle forward through
rotting, dead tissue with forked tongues.
Grumbles consumed crowds on the fringe
and depleted oil revenue.

Minimalism:
A Handbook of Minimalist Genre Poetic Forms

This handbook contains articles about how to write various minimalist poetry forms such as scifaiku, senryu, sijo, haibun, empat perkataan, ghazals, cinquain, cherita, rengays, rengu, octains, tanka, threesomes, and many more. Each article is written by an expert in that particular poetry form.

Teri Santitoro, aka sakyu, who assembled this handbook, has been the editor of Scifaikuest since 2003.

https://www.hiraethsffh.com/product-page/minimalism-a-handbook-of-minimalist-genre-poetic-forms

Featured Poet: Jane Stuart

Assisted living tree
Dry yellow leaves falling
Empty boughs forlorn

In the foyer
Two spirits
Remember mistletoe

I study
the Word
while you recite the alphabet

imagination
recreates
what wasn't there

tonight's sugar moon
falls in love
under a heavy sky

and strong, free wind
that whispers softly
to the stars, "goodbye—

to winter dreams
and silly things
that never did come true"

Going Back to the Future

My child, I've come
To take you home—
Listen to my heart
There is snow
In the mountains
And frost on the moon—
Our stars are eternal
And white
Our dove flies away
To follow the sun
You give me the warmth
Of your hand
We take our love
Back through time
Through forever
And never land

White Gardenia

A white gardenia
Squeezes its perfume
Into night's shadows
Lost in dreams
We remember time

Sleeping Forever

The little ghost
That follows me
Through green waves
Of grass
Up to a brass-lipped sky
Across the moon
And sundry stars
Believes in
An eternity of hours
And sleep inside
A box of weathered pine
Until, our hands outstretched,
We find tomorrow
Waiting to welcome
Us back into the pulsing,
Purple hour
Of twilight
When we move
A little nearer
To what we'll find
When our ghost pulls
The wagon
Nearer home

Stardust

A pocketful of stardust turns a world
Of shadows into a carpet fringed with memory
And more decision—who cares about tomorrow?
We do. We did. We try to reach the sun
To bathe in its oblivion
But it isn't possible to make those giant steps
And leave Earth behind

This Magic Night (Ojani)

This magic night,
Ojani,
Makes the moon rise,
Softly, wisely
Center of the sky
And middle of our universe
Joined by a silver thread
To Earth below
Where we wait for
Tomorrow's wings
To carry us beyond
A distant song,
A happy dance,
An opening flower,
A world beyond

When Death Is Near

It is time to turn and die
As it was once time
To twist and be born—
Freefalling into madness
Jumping into heights
Not known before
Landing on a screen of light
That pulls us homeward
Toward heaven
And the gates of Eden—
It's not a truckstop, Lord—
Out of madness intp
The glory that is waiting—
The road together

Shadows on the wall
A glass ball floating
From your universe to mine—
When winter ends
I will go back to Luxor

Śrī (Skyclad)
~ n a spencer

At a single touch
The moment of grace
A flash
       like lightning
And then release
As my body turns to rain
And the river of my dreams
                amṛta
For the mouth of an omnivorous God

My heart breaks
          as if molting
Outgrowing its skin
And opening
       like the sky
To starry chasms
Out of reach of the clouds

Where
      at the threshold
      giving birth
To the light and stellar winds
You show yourself
              just a glimpse
Of your naked skin
And mine

adjust to walking
in parallel universe
knees bend other way

    Denny E. Marshall

remove from wall
just like the previous week
a time traveler

    Denny E. Marshall

the wind
distant whispers
cryptic message alights
mysterious audience shared
tell more

    Richard E Schell

at night
an android dreams
living as a human
with memories of first being
in love

    Richard E Schell

Movie review: Godzilla Minus One

Balancing sentiment and spectacle, new Godzilla film transcends genre

Lee Clark Zumpe

Somehow, my father knew I'd be drawn to the horror genre even before it was completely evident to me — or perhaps he instilled my love for classic horror movies. He grew up during the golden age of Universal Monsters: He was 7 years old when both "Dracula" and "Frankenstein" debuted in theaters, and over the next few years, he would have seen "The Mummy," "Island of Lost Souls," "The Invisible Man," "The Bride of Frankenstein" and "Werewolf of London," among others. He also would have seen RKO's "King Kong."

So, it is no surprise that he encouraged me to watch "Creature Feature" when it premiered in 1973 on WTOG in the Tampa Bay market. Hosted by Dr. Paul Bearer — as portrayed by Dick Bennick Sr. — the locally produced series presented all of those classic horror films on Saturday afternoons.

It's also no surprise he bought me a copy of "Monsters on the Prowl," issue 29, in 1975, featuring the cover story "A Monster at My Window! with art by Jack Kirby. And it's no surprise he chose, as my first model kit, Aurora's glow-in-the-dark Godzilla.

When my father was searching for a name for his new sailboat, I suggested "Calico," the name of the research vessel in the 1978 Hanna-Barbera animated series "Godzilla." The name stuck.

Godzilla first appeared in the 1954 Japanese epic kaiju film directed by Ishirō Honda. Two years later, the Americanized version premiered in U.S. theaters. Titled "Godzilla, King of the Monsters!", the film featured original footage produced by Toho Co. Ltd., along with new footage produced by Jewell Enterprises. In addition to cast members from the original, the American adaptation adds Raymond Burr as journalist Steve Martin.

The original film spawned a media franchise that has flourished for decades. Godzilla has been showcased in more than 30 feature films. A pop culture icon and internationally recognized intellectual property, the character has also appeared in television series, novels, comic books, manga, and video games. To mark the franchise's 70th anniversary, Toho Studios and Robot Communications released "Godzilla Minus One" in Japan on Nov. 3. Toho's American subsidiary Toho International released the film in North American on Dec. 1 with English subtitles.

By way of disclaimer, I reiterate: I am a lifelong fan of horror and Godzilla holds a special place in my heart because the character is intertwined with my childhood memories. Having said that, my recommendation is that you immediately purchase tickets to see "Godzilla Minus One" in theaters, even if you have never seen a Godzilla movie and are unfamiliar with the franchise.

For those of you who have seen a Godzilla film — from the Shōwa era Toho iterations to the recent American films produced by Legendary Pictures, such as 2019's "Godzilla: King of Monsters" or 2021's "Godzilla vs. Kong" — approach this new film with the understanding that it is different than anything you have come to expect from a kaiju movie. "Godzilla

Minus One" is a surprisingly emotional story, delving deep into relatable themes focusing on the human spirit and survival in times of uncertainty and tragedy. Profoundly resonant and candidly expressive in its condemnation of war and epistemic hubris, the films succeed at something many films in the franchise fail to do: It makes you care about the well-being of its central characters.

Written and directed by Takashi Yamazaki, "Godzilla Minus One" opens in 1945 in the closing days of World War II. Kamikaze Kōichi Shikishima (Ryunosuke Kamiki), separates from his squadron and lands on Odo Island, claiming technical issues. In fact, he has chosen to disobey orders because he does not want to die.

The mechanics on the island find nothing wrong with the plane, and the lead mechanic Sōsaku Tachibana (Munetaka Aoki) guesses Kōichi's true motive. That night, Godzilla comes ashore and attacks the island outpost. Only Kōichi and Sōsaku survive, with the mechanic blaming the pilot for the deaths of his friends.

In postwar Japan, Kōichi takes refuge in the ruins of Tokyo. His parents died in the war, leaving him alone. He reluctantly takes in Noriko Ōishi (Minami Hamabe), a refugee, who is caring for an infant whose parents were killed in the bombing of Tokyo. Kōichi gradually accepts responsibility for his found family, but he is unable to explore his feelings of affection for them because he is ashamed of what he perceives as his cowardice. Burdened by survivor's guilt and tormented by post-traumatic stress disorder, Kōichi still manages to find work as a minesweeper, allowing him to support Noriko and Akiko (Sae Nagatani).

With the country still reeling from defeat in the war, Godzilla — now mutated by U.S. atomic tests at Bikini Atoll — reemerges and goes on the offensive. After destroying several U.S. naval vessels, the monster targets the Japanese mainland. The United States refuses to commit military support because it fears it would exacerbate existing tensions with the Soviet Union. Instead, the Americans ask the Japanese government to deal with the situation, even though the Imperial Japanese Navy was decommissioned after the war.

When the Japanese government fails to defend the country, a small group of civilians and Naval veterans must formulate a plan that involves Kōichi and his friends from the minesweeping crew.

Stopping Godzilla seems like an impossible task — but living in postwar Japan is an equally arduous endeavor. For Kōichi, living is a constant struggle with a range of physical, psychological, and existential challenges to overcome. He is grieving, consumed by unwarranted but inescapable guilt, and regretful. The viewer empathizes with his anguish, hoping he will overcome the effects of trauma.

Can a monster movie be a cinematic masterpiece? Yes, apparently, it can.

"Godzilla Minus One" is an epic historical drama set in a country devastated by World War II, underscoring the inhumanity of war. It balances sentiment and spectacle, often making Godzilla an incidental aspect of the fight to endure. It is an inspirational redemption tale with well-developed characters that convey the essential elements of the human condition: mortality, anxiety, aspiration, and responsibility.

Oh, and Godzilla is absolutely terrifying. Vividly rendered, the monster is the epitome of violent, catastrophic annihilation. Godzilla is an allegory for destruction, sometimes symbolic of the wrath of nature or the horror of war. Here, the monster works as both a metaphor for unresolved trauma as well as anticipatory anxiety in a world increasingly gripped by chaos, despair, and tyranny. "Godzilla Minus One" posits that even in the most desperate times, there is reason for hope.

"Godzilla Minus One" transcends the genre. It's not just a great Godzilla film — it's one of the best films of the year.

Lee Clark Zumpe is entertainment editor at Tampa Bay Newspapers, a Tomatometer-Approved Critic, and an author of short fiction appearing in select anthologies and magazines. Follow Lee at www.patreon.com/Haunter_of_the_Bijou.

Also by Lee Clark Zumpe: Wearing Winter Gray Order here:
https://www.hiraethsffh.com/product-page/wearing-winter-gray-by-lee-clark-zumpe

62 Prospect Street
Sandy DeLuca

On Saturday afternoons
I rode a bus to the city...

On Westminster,
I'd climb three flights to Madame Zell's
curtained room...
card reading for a buck.
two quarters for a bag of herbs.

A hot drink
and blueberry muffins at the tearoom...
then I ascended College Hill.

I enjoyed galleries...
especially exhibits at the famous house
on Prospect Street.

Built by Richard Upton...
back in 1860.

The place is haunted...
loved by ghost hunters, mediums
and inquisitive young girls.

That day I stayed 'til dusk...
remembered stories of Upton's
spirit in the halls...
dark figure...
silent...
quickly swallowed up by shadow.

Tales of little girls playing a game.
holding mirrors in tiny hands...
hopping down the staircase backwards.
Once at the bottom,
a future husband's face would appear...
old nannies told them so...
reminded me of a coin-operated
fortune machines in the penny arcade...
spouses and lovers predicted on flimsy cards....
all for one cent...
reminded me of Madame Zell's fortunes, too.

Stories filled my head...
I'd write everything down one day,
but specters and prophecies were on my mind.

At dusk the gallery emptied,
one last look at colorful canvases...
a chance to sign the guestbook
before heading home...
maybe listen for spectral sighs...
catch a glimpse of Richard Upton.

Then, child laughter sounded...
I heard pounding down a flight of steps...
an eerie cry...
my knees buckled and I fled for the door.

Before I ran into gathering darkness...
I glimpsed a penny by the door...

a drop of blood on the stairs...

Originally published in Phantoms of Providence

Dear Editor
Matthew Wilson

I wish my name removed from your winners page
I don't care if my drawing won best comic villain
I did not send it to the fiction quarter of still life
I drew it from my mirror and take great offence.
I do not care of the money the character would make
Some cackling villain that your superhero could
    pulverise
I cannot help how many heads I am born with, Sir
My reputation is worth more than your barbed
    compliments.
My mandibles have turned many a girl's yellow eye-
    stalks
My paint coloured scales are a testament to my work
    ethic
I will not have you lessen my efforts to "comic baddie
    of the week"
Remove my name from your winners list and publish
    no image.
My father was the first mantis to have his head eaten
    back home
I am something of a catch and hold my artwork quite
    highly
I repeat my submission was sent to the wrong
    department
Dear editor, I demand satisfaction or my name is not
    xxhhdhdsg.

Demons
Ray Greenblatt

The demons rise at night
they slither through your bloodstream
they clamber in your brain—

they show movies
of your worst moments,
the reek of brimstone
the clacking of the
antique projector—

so rhythmic it dawns
that you really do snore
after all these years
such vivid objective truth—

all these recordings
of your paltry excuses
of your arch denials
echo in the blackness
of this room, this pit
you once thought of as safe.

Immolation
~ n a spencer

This universe ... ever was, is, and will be an ever-living Fire ...
~ Herakleitos

If from Fire we come
To the Fire we return
                        even if
Falling
    ever falling
    with burning wings

We are forever sloughing time
As the dying embers of ourselves

Glowing through the ash
                      bright sentience
                      too hot to hold

But burning
        ever burning
Perpetually falling freely
With nowhere to land
                    but the burning
Bright radiance of sense and longing
Covered over in ashen pride

                    and vain regret
                       all hope forsaking
Afire
      these wings are burning
And I am falling like a meteor
                              into
                              and out of nowhere

The Future Adventures of
Bailey Belvedere

https://www.hiraethsffh.com/product-page/further-adventures-of-bailey-belvedere-by-tyree-campbell

Light the Second Sun
Amanda Niamh Dawson

Get to work
Lots to be done
Harness hyperspace
Weave frequencies into lace
Projections reach darkest space
Spinning spheres
Swarming years
Overlapping seams
Cosmic eaves
No dark side
Illumination by guides
Electric currents lie

Ignited
Both eyes blinded

After Mom's Divorce
Matthew Wilson

The first day at school is a nightmare
To see what horror this transfer brings
Stressing how you forgot your lunch
To share among new friends with wings
Teasing is only natural for the new kid
With just ten fingers and two eyes
But true friends help with maths tests
And soar a shortcut through the skies.
The girl with tentacles asks to dance
And steal a kiss by the green moon
But mother said that change is good
Her new job starting soon.
The funny money has two heads here
But mom's wages will buy a place
If you make a go at making friends
Even with no tentacles upon your face.

plenum
Peter Roberts

our multiverse is so diverse –
10^50 different sorts – yet
all just variants on a theme –
a few tweaked parameters.

but could there be something
beyond all that, something
truly other? orthogonal to
what we could ever imagine?

a place without dimensions?
or a universe alogical?

or could it be whatever place
that we can't think to think of?

Border Story
~ n a spencer

My vocabulary did this to me ...
~ Jack Spicer

I'll turn it all in
               and over
Stored up in fragments against the wrack
And erasures of a mortal endurance

Slowly slipping grasp
                       these scattered traces
Constellated against a discrepant horizon

In a body of words
                 and porous recollection
Look for me there
                 in the windy
                           open spaces

www.ingramcontent.com/pod-product-compliance
Lightning Source LLC
LaVergne TN
LVHW021953060526
838201LV00049B/1689